W9-AUR-477

DON:
10-96

"This Land Is Your Land"
Let's Explore
the Pacific West

Jill C. Wheeler

Published by Abdo & Daughters, 4940 Viking Drive, Suite 622, Edina, MN 55435.

Library bound edition distributed by Rockbottom Books, Pentagon Tower, P.O. Box 36036, Minneapolis, Minnesota 55435.

Photos by:
Bettmann Archives: 4, 7, 9, 16, 17, 18, 19, 23, 24
Archive Photos: 4, 5, 8, 9, 10, 13, 14, 17, 22
Wide World Photos: 5, 6, 7, 8, 14, 16, 17, 20, 21
John Hamilton: 3, 5, 11, 12, 14, 15

Edited by John Hamilton

Library of Congress Cataloging–in–Publication Data
Wheeler, Jill C., 1964-
    The Pacific West / Jill C. Wheeler.
        p.   cm — (America, this land is your land)
    Includes bibliographical references and index.
    ISBN 1-56239-299-9
    1. Northwest, Pacific—Juvenile literature. 2. Hawaii—Juvenile
literature. 3. Alaska—Juvenile literature. I. Title. II. Series:
Wheeler, Jill c., 1964- America, this land is your land.
F852.3.W44   1994
917.95—dc20   94-18504
                CIP
                AC

Contents

Let's Explore The Pacific West 4

Historical Highlights 6

Lay Of The Land 10

Plants & Animals 14

Famous Folks 16

Favorite Cities 20

Fast Facts 25

Suggestions For Further Reading 29

Glossary 30

Index 32

◀ Kalalau Valley, part of
the breathtaking Na Pali
Coast on the island of
Kauai, Hawaii.

Let's Explore the Pacific West

Where in the United States can you find *volcanoes*? Where can you see brightly colored desert canyons? Where can you swim on a tropical beach? If you said the Pacific West, you're right.

The Pacific West has many kinds of places. It includes the frozen *tundra* of Alaska. It has sweltering deserts in Arizona and California. It is home to the Great Salt Lake and the black sand beaches of Hawaii. Visitors can find almost any landscape they want in the Pacific West.

These wonders have attracted many people over the years. Explorers were

▲ *Hot lava erupts from Hawaii's Mount Kilauea volcano.*

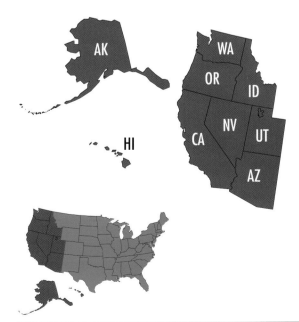

▲ *The completion of the first transcontinental railroad in Promontory, UT, on May 10, 1869.*

◄ *California contains beautiful coastal scenery, and is also home to the entertainment industry.*

the first Europeans to see this incredible land. They came to find gold and other riches. They told others about their discoveries. Religious leaders came soon after. They came to teach Native Americans about their religion. Then white settlers arrived. Some settlers wanted riches, too. Others only wanted to practice their religion.

It was hard for people to get to the Pacific West. People coming from the east had to cross high mountains. People coming from the west crossed miles of ocean. Many people died on the journey. Those who arrived faced other problems. These included earthquakes and storms.

In time, a railroad stretched from California to New York. Then workers built the *Panama Canal*. The canal made it easier for people to sail to the Pacific Coast from the Atlantic Coast. It was much easier for people to reach the Pacific West now. This helped the

area grow. Later, airplanes made the journey from West Coast to Hawaii. This also helped the Hawaiian Islands grow.

World War II also spurred growth in the Pacific West. The military sent many soldiers to places like California and Hawaii. Workers built *factories* to make planes and ships. Some of the soldiers and workers stayed in the Pacific West after the war. They built homes and businesses.

The Pacific West is still a special region. People from all over the world visit its unique places like Hollywood, Waikiki Beach, and the Grand Canyon. Like the first settlers, they come for adventure and excitement. As before, the Pacific West never disappoints.

▲ *Washington's Olympic National Park.*

5

Historical Highlights

The Pacific West was the last frontier of the United States. It contains the nation's two youngest states. These states are Alaska and Hawaii. Many events in the Pacific West happened less than 150 years ago. This may seem like a long time ago. Yet it is a short time compared to other U.S. regions. Let's look at how recent these events are:

▲ *Prospectors panning for gold in the Pacific West.*

700-1200 The *Pueblo* people flourish in Arizona.

1540 Spanish explorer Francisco Vasquez de Coronado enters Arizona.

1579 English explorer Sir Francis Drake explores the California coast. He claims the land for England.

1602 Spanish explorer Sebastián Vizcaíno visits California. He urges Spain to settle the new land.

1741 Danish explorer Vitus Bering reaches Alaska. It is his second voyage. He explores the area for Russia.

1769 Spanish priest Junipero Serra begins a *mission* in California. He calls it San Diego de Alcalá.

1778 Englishman James Cook discovers the Hawaiian Islands. He names them the Sandwich Islands.

1784 Russian traders start a settlement in Alaska. They call it Kodiak.

1795 King Kamehameha I conquers all but two of the Hawaiian islands.

1809 Explorer David Thompson begins a trading post in Idaho. The post is for the Hudson Bay Company.

1810 British and Canadian traders begin a fur-trading post. It is near Spokane, Washington. King Kamehameha I unites all Hawaiian islands.

1820 Missionaries arrive in Hawaii. They want to teach the Hawaiians about Christianity.

1822 Mexico takes over California.

1841 The first overland wagon train arrives in California. The settlers have traveled on the *Oregon Trail*.

1846 Heavy snows strand a group of settlers in Donner Pass, Nevada. Only about half of the settlers live to reach California.

1847 Brigham Young leads the first group of *Mormons* to Utah. They settle by the Great Salt Lake.

◀ *Thousands of gold-seekers cross Alaska to the Canadian Klondike.*

▼ *The Panama Canal under construction in 1913.*

Hoover Dam is completed in 1936. ▶

1848 Mexico gives California, Nevada, Utah and Arizona to the United States. *Prospectors* find gold Sutter's Mill, California.

1849 Thousands of prospectors hurry to California. They are looking for gold.

1850 California becomes a state.

1855-58 Soldiers and Native Americans fight in Washington. The Native Americans do not want to give up their homeland.

1859 Prospectors discover silver in Nevada. They call the place Comstock.

1862 *Confederate* soldiers take over Tucson. Native Americans and U.S. soldiers fight the Battle of Apache Pass in Arizona. Cochise and Mangas Coloradas lead the Native American forces.

1864 Nevada becomes a state.

1867 The United States buys Alaska from Russia. The land costs $7.2 million.

1869 Workers complete the first *transcontinental railroad*. The workers drive the last spike in Utah.

1877 Nez Perce Chief Joseph surrenders. Soldiers force him and his people to a *reservation* in Idaho.

1886 Apache leader Geronimo surrenders. The surrender ends wars between soldiers and Native Americans.

1889 Washington becomes a state.

1890 Idaho becomes a state.

1893 Hawaiians revolt. They overthrow Queen Liliuokalani. They create a temporary *republic*.

1896 Thousands of prospectors cross Alaska to the Canadian Klondike. They are seeking gold. Utah becomes a state.

1899 Prospectors discover oil in Bakersfield, California.

1900 Hawaii becomes a U.S. territory.

1903 Workers pack the first Hawaiian pineapple.

◀ *The aftermath of the terrible 1906 San Francisco earthquake.*

◄ A ship explodes during the Japanese attack on Pearl Harbor, Hawaii.

1906 A terrible earthquake hits San Francisco.

1912 Arizona becomes the 48th state.

1914 The first ships use the Panama Canal.

1927 Hawaiians welcome the first flight to arrive from the mainland.

1931 Gambling is legalized in Nevada.

1936 Workers finish the great Hoover Dam.

1941 Japanese soldiers attack Pearl Harbor, Hawaii. The attack takes U.S. soldiers by surprise. The battle forces the U.S. into World War II.

1942 Japanese soldiers capture three Aleutian Islands near Alaska. U.S. soldiers quickly get the islands back.

1945 Diplomats found the United Nations in San Francisco.

1959 Hawaii becomes the 50th state.

1977 Workers complete the *Trans Alaska Pipeline*.

1980 Mount St. Helens erupts in Washington.

1984 The summer Olympic games come to Los Angeles.

1989 The *Exxon Valdez* oil tanker runs aground in Alaska. It spills oil in Prince William Sound. It is one of the world's worst ecological disasters. The same year, another terrible earthquake strikes San Francisco.

Mount St. Helens blows its top, 1980. ►

Lay of the Land

It's impossible to describe the Pacific West in a few words. The region offers many different climates and landscapes.

The eastern part of the Pacific West features rugged mountains, dry plateaus and deserts. This is the western side of the Rocky Mountains. Mighty rivers run through these lands. They include the Colorado River. This giant river has carved out hundreds of miles of canyons. You can visit the canyons in Utah and Arizona.

To the northwest, plateaus give way to the Cascade Mountains.

▼ *Alaska's Mount McKinley.*

▲ *The Grand Canyon of northern Arizona. This photo was taken at sunset from Cape Royal on the north rim.*

Hawaii is known for its beaches and ▶ *warm blue waters.*

The Pacific Ocean lies west of these mountains. The ocean and mountains combine to create lush forests in Washington and Oregon. The mighty Columbia and Snake Rivers have carved canyons in these lands.

California is a mixture of landscapes. Northern shores are mild and rainy. Farther south, the land turns hot and dry. Alaska and Hawaii are nearly as different as two places can be. Most of Alaska is cold. Hawaii is a tropical paradise. It's not surprising the Pacific West is home to so many natural wonders. Following are just a few:

◀ *The lush forests of Washington. West of the Cascade Mountains, plentiful rainfall creates vast areas of old-growth forest. In Olympic National Park, where these photos were taken, some areas get so much rain that they are classified as rainforest.*

Waikiki Beach is on the Hawaiian island of Oahu. Its white sands and warm blue waters attracts thousands of visitors. The water is perfect for sailing, swimming and surfing. Nearby is **Diamond Head**. Diamond Head is an old volcanic crater.

An extinct volcano created **Crater Lake** in Oregon. Crater Lake is the deepest lake in the United States. Its icy waters are 1,932 feet deep. The water in the lake has nowhere to go.

The **Canyonlands** and **Grand Canyon** are in southern Utah and northern Arizona. Thousands of visitors marvel at Zion and Bryce Canyons in Utah. These parks feature colorful rock formations. Rivers, wind and rain have carved and sculpted these formations. The Grand Canyon is the largest canyon of all.

Washington's **Mount St. Helens** made history in 1980. The volcano erupted for the first time in 123 years. The eruption sent ash 11 miles into the air. The ash fell back down on the surrounding land. The eruption from Mount St. Helens covered some nearby towns with up to seven inches of ash.

▲ *Oregon's Crater Lake, the deepest lake in the United States.*

Death Valley in California is the lowest place in the United States. It is 282 feet below sea level. Death Valley only gets about three inches of rain a year. Recordkeepers recorded the nation's highest temperature there. It reached 134 degrees Fahrenheit.

Yosemite National Park is another California attraction. It has beautiful rock formations, redwood trees and waterfalls. The highest waterfall is Ribbon Falls. It is the highest waterfall in the nation.

The **Great Salt Lake** is an inland sea in Utah. It is up to eight times saltier than any ocean. People swimming in it can float easily. This is because of all the salt. The lake covers more than 2,000 square miles.

▲ *Yosemite National Park in California.*

▼ *California's Death Valley is the lowest place on Earth at 282 feet below sea level.*

Plants & Animals

Think about the land of the Pacific West. It is very different from place to place. It's not surprising that the plants and animals are also different.

Hawaii has a tropical climate. The warm, wet weather produces lush plants and flowers. There are 650 species of plants found only in Hawaii. These include dark red anthuriums and the rare silversword plant. Hawaii also is home to thousands of orchids and

▲ *The hala (hah-lah) tree of Hawaii. Its fruit is often mistaken for pineapple.*

hibiscus. The nene lives among these plants and huge fern trees. It is a rare Hawaiian goose. Edible plants include the pineapple, coconut, guava and ti. People make grass skirts from ti leaves. Many game fish, such as marlin and swordfish, live off the coast.

The climate is very different in Alaska. The arctic cold is home to fur-bearing animals. These include

◀ *Humpback whales and polar bear are found in Alaska. (Whales also migrate to Hawaii.)*

◀ *A white-tailed ptarmigan, a member of the grouse family. They are common in the mountains of Alaska and Washington.*

◀ *Indian paintbrush, a common flower in the mountains.*

Farther south, the vegetation changes as the land turns dry and rocky. Many kinds of cacti live here. The cacti include the saguaro and the Joshua tree. The Joshua tree can grow to be 25 feet tall. Desert animals include the Gila monster, tortoises and coyote.

polar bears, kodiak bears, wolverines, wolves and fur seals. Sea otters, whales and walruses make their home in the cold waters here. Salmon and halibut also live there. The Alaskan landscape has two seasons. In winter, snow covers much of the land. Short summers bring a carpet of wildflowers and grasses.

On the mainland, you can see bald eagles in Washington. They live among thick forests of Douglas fir and Sitka spruce. The many lakes of the Northwest are home to marmots, otters and beavers. Elk and deer roam the western side of the Cascade Mountains. Sea lions and salmon live in nearby waters, too. The Indian paintbrush is one of many mountain wildflowers.

The deserts of southern California change to lush redwood forests in the north. Some of the world's oldest and tallest trees live here. These magnificent trees grow up to 275 feet tall.

The mountains of this region have their own unique residents. Mountain lions, bighorn sheep and pronghorn antelope live here. Buffalo still roam some of the flatter lands as well.

◀ *A saguaro cactus, found in the deserts of Arizona.*

Famous Folks

Many famous people call the Pacific West home. Everyone knows Hollywood, California, for its movie stars. Yet other kinds of people also have lived in the Pacific West. Brave Native Americans. Rugged explorers. Talented athletes. And successful politicians.

The people of the Pacific West also have a rich blend of backgrounds. They include Native American and Polynesian peoples, plus Europeans. Following is a look at some of these people who have their roots in this land:

Sandra Day O'Connor (1930-) O'Connor made history in 1981. She became the first woman to sit on the U.S. Supreme Court. She is from Arizona.

John Elway (1960-) This famous quarterback is from Port Angeles, Washington. He has led teams to many Super Bowl games. Some people say he is one of the best quarterbacks in the National Football League.

Cochise (1812?-1874) Cochise was a brave Native American leader. Soldiers killed some of his family for a crime they did not commit. Cochise fought against the soldiers to get revenge. He was from what is now the state of Arizona.

Barry Goldwater (1909-   )  Goldwater began his career as a shopkeeper. Then he became a U.S. Senator. He ran for president in 1964 but lost. Ronald Reagan used many of Goldwater's ideas later. Goldwater was from Phoenix, Arizona.

Jack London (1876-1916) London wrote more than 40 books. He was born in San Francisco, California. He spent much of his time on the waterfront. Many of his books deal with water and nature.

Richard Nixon (1913-1994) Nixon was the nation's 37th president. He helped the U.S. improve relations with China and Russia. He resigned in 1974 after the Watergate scandal. He was born in Yorba Linda, CA.

John Steinbeck (1902-1968) Steinbeck was a famous novelist. He set many of his novels in his native California. He won the Nobel Prize for Literature in 1962.

Geronimo (1829-1909) Geronimo was an Apache Indian leader. He was born in what is now the state of Arizona. He led many daring raids against white soldiers. The raids were so his people could keep their land. He later turned himself in to the soldiers. He spent his final days on a reservation. ▼

Chief Joseph (1840?-1904) Chief Joseph was a Native American leader. His people were the Nez Perce. He fought to keep Nez Perce lands, but soldiers forced them to live on a reservation. He was born in what is today the state of Idaho.

Sarah Winnemucca (1844-1891) Winnemucca was a Paiute Indian. She learned English as a young girl. She worked as an interpreter between her people and the whites. She tried to help her people keep their lands. She was from Humboldt Lake, Nevada.

Linus Pauling (1901-) Pauling is one of the only people to win two Nobel Prizes. He won one for chemistry. He also won the Nobel Peace Prize. He was born in Portland, Oregon.

Mary Decker Slaney (1958-) Slaney is a runner. She has set many records in track events. She competed in the 1984 and 1988 Olympics. She's from Eugene, OR.

Robert Frost (1874-1963) Frost was a famous poet. He spent much of

his life in New England. However, he was born in San Francisco, California. He won three Pulitzer Prizes. He taught poetry at Harvard University.

Earl Warren (1891-1974) Warren was born in Los Angeles, California. He practiced law in California. Then he became the state's attorney general and governor. In 1953, he became the Chief Justice of the U.S. Supreme Court.

General George Patton (1885-1945) Patton gained fame during World War II. His bravery earned him the nickname "Old Blood and Guts." He was from San Gabriel, California.

Chief Seattle (1786?-1866) Chief Seattle was a wise Native American leader. He was born in what is now Washington state. He gave a famous speech in 1854. The speech told about how Europeans would soon take over Native American lands.

Ahmad Rashad (1949-) Rashad is a well known sportscaster. Before that, he played professional football. He is from Portland, Oregon.

Beverly Cleary (1916-) Cleary has written many children's books. Her characters include Ramona Quimby and Henry Huggins. She grew up in McMinnville, Oregon.

King Kamehameha I (1758?-1819) Kamehameha was a brave warrior. He was born on the island of Hawaii. Eventually, he conquered all the Hawaiian islands. He united the islands this way.

Don Ho (1924-) People around the world know this popular singer. He has introduced many people to Hawaiian music. He is from Honolulu, Hawaii.

John Moses Browning (1855-1926) Browning was a gunsmith. He invented several guns, including the Browning automatic rifle. He was from Provo, Utah.

Donny Osmond (1958-) and **Marie Osmond** (1959-) are singers from Ogden, Utah. They had their own TV show from 1976-1979. They also performed with other members of their family.

Bing Crosby (1904-1977) Crosby was a popular singer and actor. He starred in more than 50 movies. He was born in Tacoma, Washington.

Gary Larson (1950-) Many people enjoy Larson's comic strip. It is called "The Far Side." He is from Tacoma, Washington.

Marilyn Monroe (1926-1962) Monroe was an actress and model from Los Angeles, California. She starred in 30 films. She died when she was only 36 years old. ▼

Favorite Cities

▲ *Los Angeles seems to glow under a lunar eclipse.*

The cities of the Pacific West are a delight to visit. You can find everything from movie stars to museums. Here are highlights of a few of these great cities:

Los Angeles

People around the world know **Los Angeles, California**. It is home to Hollywood. This is the nation's filmmaking and television capital. The city also has many beaches, amusement parks and museums.

Native Americans were the first people in Los Angeles. Then, Spanish explorers discovered the area. They gave it a Spanish name meaning "River Town of Our Lady, the Queen of the Angels." The city still has many places with Spanish names.

In the early 1900s, prospectors discovered oil near Los Angeles. Many people moved to the city to make their fortunes. Later, the film industry began. The city grew again during World War II. It became a *manufacturing* center for aircraft. The aircraft industry is still an important part of the city.

Las Vegas

Las Vegas, Nevada, is a world-famous resort city. Millions of people visit each year to gamble at Las Vegas casinos. Other nearby attractions are Hoover Dam and giant Lake Mead. Las Vegas also is the commercial center for local mining and ranching activities.

California-bound settlers were the first whites to visit Las Vegas. The settlers stopped to use local springs. Mormons also lived in Las Vegas briefly. The modern city began in 1864. The Army built a fort there that year.

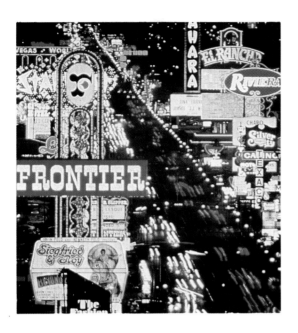

▲ Las Vegas shimmers in the desert night, lit by millions of fluorescent and neon bulbs outside its many casinos, clubs and restaurants.

Seattle

Seattle, Washington, sits between Puget Sound and the Cascade Mountains. The climate is mild and rainy. Rain falls about 150 days each year.

Shipping has long been an important industry in Seattle. Aircraft and wood products manufacturing are important, too. The Boeing aircraft company has been in Seattle since the 1920s. The city also has professional football, baseball and basketball teams.

In 1905, the railroad reached Las Vegas. The railroad brought many more people to live in Las Vegas. The city grew even more after gambling became legal in 1931.

Tragedy struck the city in 1980. A fire at the MGM Grand Hotel killed 84 people.

White settlers founded Seattle in 1851. They named the city after a local Native American chief. The city began as a lumber town. Later, the new railroad and the Yukon gold rush both helped the city grow. During World War II, Seattle became an important shipbuilding and aircraft center.

In 1962, Seattle hosted the World's Fair. One of the Fair's attractions was the Space Needle. Tourists still visit this 607-foot-tall structure. The Seattle Art Museum is another attraction.

Honolulu

Honolulu, Hawaii, is one of the world's most popular places to visit. Tourists can see natural wonders like Waikiki Beach and Diamond Head. They also may visit the historic Iolani Palace, where Hawaiian royalty once lived. Other attractions are the Foster Botanic Gardens and the Honolulu Zoo.

Legend says people first lived in Honolulu around 1100. This makes it the oldest city in the United States. The first European to enter Honolulu Harbor was Captain

▲ *Honolulu, the capital of Hawaii.*

William Brown. He arrived in 1794. Honolulu became the capital of the Hawaiian kingdom in 1845. In 1942, Japanese soldiers bombed Honolulu's Pearl Harbor.

Today, many Honolulu factories process sugar and can pineapple. Tourism also is important. The U.S. Pacific Command headquarters are in Honolulu as well.

Anchorage

Anchorage, Alaska, is the state's largest city. It sits on a bay of the

Pacific Ocean. The Chugach Mountains are nearby. Anchorage is a center for local oil, shipping, coal and natural gas industries.

The Alaska Railroad started Anchorage as a construction base in 1914. World War II helped the city grow. Anchorage became home to a large fort and air force base. Today, it is home to Alaska Pacific University and the University of Alaska at Anchorage as well.

In 1964, a major earthquake rocked the city. The quake was the second most severe recorded in the world.

San Francisco

San Francisco, California, sits on one of the world's largest bays. The famous Golden Gate Bridge crosses this bay. Alcatraz Island sits in the bay. The buildings on the island used to be a prison. In the bay, currents are strong and cold.

Spanish settlers arrived in San Francisco in 1776. They built a fort called the Presidio, which is still used today. Other tourist attractions include cable cars, Fisherman's Wharf and Chinatown.

▼ *San Francisco's Golden Gate Bridge.*

Many of San Francisco's early residents were *immigrants*. They came from places like China, Italy and Russia. In 1906 a major earthquake hit the city. San Francisco has earthquakes every once in a while. It sits on the *San Andreas Fault*.

Phoenix

Phoenix, Arizona, is the state's capital and largest city. It sits on the Salt River. It has a dry, warm climate. The climate attracts many new residents each year. In fact, the population grew more than fifteenfold between 1940 and 1990.

Phoenix began as an agricultural center. Local farmers grew citrus fruits, cotton and cattle. Today, aerospace, chemicals and textiles are important industries. Phoenix also is a key transportation center.

Native Americans were the first to live in Phoenix. They built an *irrigation* system in 1867. The irrigation system attracted white settlers to the area. The city began officially in 1881. A railroad reached it in 1887.

▼ *In summer, Phoenix bakes under the desert sun.*

Fast Facts

Alaska

Population: 560,000
Area: 591,000 square miles
Capital: Juneau
Industries: Fishing, furs, game, gas, lumber, oil, tourism, wood products.
State Flower: Forget-me-not
State Bird: Willow ptarmigan
Statehood Date: January 3, 1959

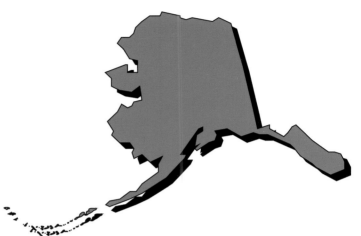

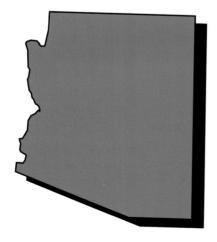

Arizona

Population: 3.7 million
Area: 114,000 square miles
Capital: Phoenix
Industries: Aerospace, agriculture, manufacturing, mining.
State Flower: Blossom of the saguaro cactus
State Bird: Cactus wren
Statehood Date: February 14, 1912

California

Population: 29.8 million
Area: 158,706 square miles
Capital: Sacramento
Industries: Aerospace, agriculture, electronics, fishing, manufacturing, tourism.
State Flower: Golden poppy
State Bird: California valley quail
Statehood Date: Sept. 9, 1850

Hawaii

Population: 1.1 million
Area: 6,471 square miles
Capital: Honolulu
Industries: Agriculture, clothing, fishing, tourism.
State Flower: Yellow hibiscus
State Bird: Hawaiian goose
Statehood Date: August 21, 1959

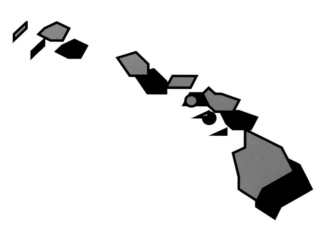

Idaho

Population: 1 million
Area: 83, 564 square miles
Capital: Boise
Industries: Agriculture, chemicals, electronics, lumber, manufacturing, mining, tourism.
State Flower: Syringa
State Bird: Mountain bluebird
Statehood Date: July 3, 1890

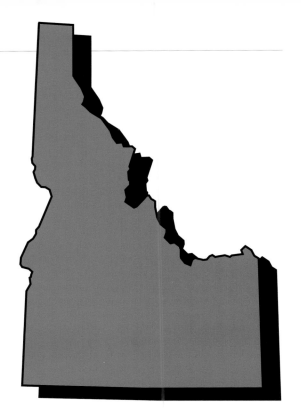

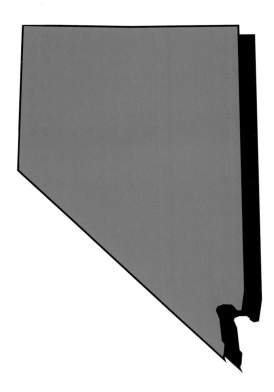

Nevada

Population: 1.2 million
Area: 110, 561 square miles
Capital: Carson City
Industries: Agriculture, gambling, manufacturing, mining, tourism.
State Flower: Sagebrush
State Bird: Mountain bluebird
Statehood Date: October 31, 1864

Oregon

Population: 2.8 million
Area: 97,073 square miles
Capital: Salem
Industries: Agriculture, food processing, forestry, manufacturing, printing.
State Flower: Oregon grape
State Bird: Western meadowlark
Statehood Date: February 14, 1859

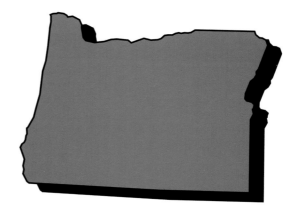

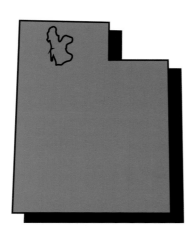

Utah

Population: 1.7 million
Area: 84,899 square miles
Capital: Salt Lake City
Industries: Construction, defense products, electronics, manufacturing, mining.
State Flower: Sego lily
State Bird: Sea gull
Statehood Date: January 4, 1896

Washington

Population: 4.9 million
Area: 68,139 square miles
Capital: Olympia
Industries: Aerospace, agriculture, fishing, food products, forest products, paper.
State Flower: Western rhododendron
State Bird: Willow goldfinch
Statehood Date: Nov. 11, 1889

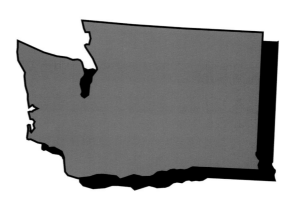

Suggestions For Further Reading

Kids Learn America by Patricia Gordon and Reed C. Snow, Williamsburg Publishing Co.

Children's Atlas of the United States, Rand McNally & Company.

All About Our 50 States by Margaret Ronan, Random House.

Going West: Cowboys and Pioneers by Martine Courtault, Marboro Books.

Gold! The Klondike Adventure by Delia Ray, Lodestar Books.

A Frontier Fort On The Oregon Trail by Scott Steedman and Mark Bergen, Peter Bedrick Books.

Kidding Around Los Angeles by Judy Cash, John Muir Publications.

Kidding Around San Francisco by Rosemary Zibart, John Muir Publications.

Kidding Around The National Parks of the Southwest by Sarah Lovett, John Muir Publications.

Glossary

Confederate
Name given to the Southern states during the United States Civil War.

Factories
Places where people make products.

Immigrants
People who move to a foreign country and settle there.

Irrigation
Watering land by sending water through canals, ditches or pipes.

Manufacturing
To make products from raw materials.

Mission
A settlement started by a religious group.

Mormons
People who practice the Mormon religion.

Oregon Trail
A route traveled by settlers moving West. It started in Missouri and ended in Oregon. It crossed 2,000 miles of prairie, mountains and desert. It took between four and six months to cross by covered wagon.

Panama Canal
A waterway connecting the Atlantic and Pacific Oceans.

Prospectors
People who looked for gold and other minerals.

Pueblo
An Indian tribe that lived in the West many years ago.

Republic
A form of government that does not use kings and queens.

Reservation
A place where the government sent Native Americans to live.

San Andreas Fault
A break in the Earth's crust. The San Andreas is the largest fault in the nation.

Trans Alaska Pipeline
An 800-mile pipeline for transporting oil. The pipeline runs from Alaska's North Slope to Prince William Sound.

Transcontinental Railroad
The first railroad to join the Atlantic and Pacific Coasts.

Tundra
A treeless plain in the arctic.

Volcano
A hole in the Earth's surface that shoots out molten rock and steam.

Index

A

Anchorage (AK)   22, 23

B

Bering, Vitus   6
Browning, John Moses   19

C

Canyonlands   12
Cascades   10, 12, 15, 21
Chief Joseph   8, 18
Chief Seattle   18
Cleary, Beverly   19
Cochise   8, 16
Colorado River   10
Cook, James   6
Coronado, Francisco   6
Crater Lake   12, 13
Crosby, Bing   19

D

Death Valley   13
Donner Pass   7
Drake, Sir Francis   6

E

Elway, John   16
Exxon Valdez   9

F

Frost, Robert   18

G

Geronimo   8, 17
Gold 5, 8, 21, 23
Goldwater, Barry   17
Grand Canyon   5, 11, 12
Great Salt Lake   4, 7, 13

H

Ho, Don   19
Hollywood   5, 16, 20
Honolulu (HI)   19, 22, 26
Hoover Dam   8, 9, 20

I

Indian paintbrush   15

K

Kamehameha, King   6, 19
Klondike   7, 8, 29

L

Larson, Gary   19
Las Vegas (NV)   20, 21
London, Jack   17
Los Angeles (CA)
    9, 18, 19, 20

M

Monroe, Marilyn   19
Mount St. Helens   9, 12

N

Nixon, Richard   17

O

O'Connor, Sandra Day   16
Oregon Trail   7, 29, 30
Osmond, Donny   19
Osmond, Marie   19

P

Panama Canal   5, 9, 30
Patton, George   18
Pauling, Linus   18
Pearl Harbor   9, 22
Phoenix (AZ)   17, 24, 25
Prince William Sound   9, 31
Pueblo (CO)   6, 31

R

Rashad, Ahmad   19
Rocky Mountains   10

S

San Andreas Fault   24, 31
San Francisco (CA)
    8, 9, 17, 23
Seattle (WA)   21
Serra, Junipero   6
Slaney, Mary Decker   18
Steinbeck, John   17
Sutter's Mill   8

T

Trans Alaska Pipeline   9, 31
Transcontinental Railroad   4,
    8, 31
Tundra   4, 31

V

Volcano   4, 12, 31

W

Waikiki Beach (HI)   5, 12, 22
Warren, Earl   18
Winnemucca, Sarah   18

Y

Yosemite National Park   13
Young, Brigham   7